TEACHER TEAMWORK

How do we make it work?

Margaret
SEARLE

Marilyn
SWARTZ

 Alexandria, VA USA

Website: www.ascd.org
E-mail: books@ascd.org

www.ascdarias.org

PAPERBACK ISBN: 978-1-4166-2066-2   ASCD product # SF115045
Also available as an e-book (see Books in Print for the ISBNs).

Library of Congress Cataloging-in-Publication Data
Searle, Margaret.
  Teacher teamwork : how do we make it work? / Margaret Searle and Marilyn Swartz.
     pages cm
  Includes bibliographical references.
  ISBN 978-1-4166-2066-2 (pbk. : alk. paper) 1. Teaching teams. I. Swartz, Marilyn. II. Title.
  LB1029.T4S43 2015
  371.14'8--dc23

                         2015006552

21 20 19 18 17 16 15   1 2 3 4 5 6 7 8 9 10

TEACHER TEAMWORK

How do we make it work?

Want to earn a free ASCD Arias e-book?
Your opinion counts! Please take 2–3 minutes to give
us your feedback on this publication. All survey
respondents will be entered into a drawing to
win an ASCD Arias e-book.

Please visit
www.ascd.org/ariasfeedback

Thank you!

Introduction

The best teamwork comes from men who are working independently toward one goal in unison.

—James Cash Penney

When we asked educators across the nation the question, "How well do your teams use their common planning time?" the same issues kept popping up. "I would rather eat glass than go to a meeting at our school. It's a waste." "I need my planning time to do my own work." "If I would die during our team meeting, the transition would be very subtle. So boring!"

We know that working together can help us solve tough problems and keep our sanity at the same time. People have far more potential for reducing anxiety, addressing complex issues, and improving creativity when they work in teams, so why do many educators have such adverse reactions to teamwork? Perhaps they do not take the time to establish unity and purpose—the glue that holds a team together. Maybe they forget to apply the oil of routines, norms, and procedures to make things run smoothly.

This book will guide paraprofessionals, teachers, and supervisors through simple steps to move your school from "groups of reluctant players" to "highly effective teams." We will look at how the needs of your team change as you move through predictable stages of team development. The first section provides guidelines for setting up purpose, protocols, and norms. If you are an established team, this section will serve as a quick reminder to make certain you didn't skip any basic steps. The next section discusses ways to build the skills necessary for resolving the conflicts that eat away at team time. The following section focuses on reducing conflict through solid decision-making procedures. The last section provides strategies for building the capacity a team needs to take on tough problems.

If your teams follow this advice faithfully, ongoing frustrations about team time will be replaced by feelings of accomplishment and satisfaction. The insights and procedures in this book are simple to learn, but creating an environment of collaboration is not as easy as just knowing the steps. To build productive teams you need to intentionally create an environment of enthusiasm and engagement. So let's take a look at elements of effective teaming.

Establish Guidelines and Protocols

If everyone is moving forward together, then success takes care of itself.

—Henry Ford

Think of the most enjoyable, satisfying experience you have ever had as a team member. It may have been a choir or a sports team, a community or school group, or a club you were interested in. The team may have been two people or 22 people working together. List the qualities that made this teaming experience enjoyable and satisfying.

Even though each person's positive experience is different, the list of what makes the experience great tends to have the same basic themes. Here is a summary of the top six statements we heard from educators we surveyed:

- We worked on things so important that I knew it was worth my time and effort.
- Group members were competent and cooperative and made all members feel that they were an important part of the process.
- We were well organized, efficient, and flexible.
- We stayed committed and I was proud to be a part of the quality work that the team produced.
- Communication was honest, upbeat, and positive as well as clear and timely.
- I felt supported and grew personally as a result of being part of this team.

Things like worthy goals, sense of belonging, commitment to quality and feeling supported are the essential glue that binds a group to both the work and each other. Organization, communication, and flexibility act as the oil that reduces friction and keeps things running smoothly. Now think of your own team. How many of these statements accurately describe how members feel about your group?

Support and commitment doesn't just happen. It takes intentional work to get people to put aside self-interest and act for the good of the team. People always start out as a group of individuals and if they hang together as they go through what B.W. Tuckman calls the four stages of group development (1965) they become a highly functioning team complete with all the joy and satisfaction that implies. These four stages are Forming, Storming, Norming, and Performing.

The Forming Stage of Teaming

At first members are highly dependent upon their leader for direction. Members tend to be polite and hopeful but at the same time wary and unsure about the team and how each member fits into it. During this "getting to know you" time members are reluctant to voice differences of opinion. Controversy feels like unsafe territory because trust has yet to be established. People are unsure of the "who, what, when, where, how, and why" of the work, so they hold back on commitment until they have answers. This holding back can prevent the team from getting important work done.

What Does the Team Need At This Stage?

During the Forming Stage teams need to clarify their purpose, set up norms and procedures, and form relationships. For some teams this stage takes months and for others this stage happens quickly. Many successful groups we interviewed attributed their team's initial success to the strength of their leaders. They said that in the beginning the leaders played a critical part in helping the team get a clear mental picture of both the goal and the processes for working collaboratively. These leaders fostered team ownership of the processes as well as responsibility for the results. They focused as much on developing positive interpersonal dynamics as they did on the work at this stage. This "laying the groundwork" part of team-building often frustrates people who want to "get down to business," but it is relationships, common vision, trust, and collaborative practices that create the cornerstone for keeping morale and productivity high.

A team from Garfield Elementary in Ohio said their secret for successful teamwork was quality time. They said that a district-sponsored training launched their biggest boost in productivity. The training gave their team guidance as well as uninterrupted time to plan and get to know each other personally and professionally. Trust and a sense of purpose developed as their vision and work became clearer. A calm environment with time to talk is essential for forging relationships that result in a strong collaborative team.

Creating an Inspiring Vision

There is an old proverb that states, "A vision without a plan is just a dream. A plan without vision is just drudgery. But a vision with a plan can change the world." Research shows that having a clearly articulated high-impact vision is an essential characteristic of effective teams (Larson & LaFasto, 2001). When a team looks like it is capable of accomplishing something great and the challenge seems worth the effort, people want to be a part of it. According to our survey, lack of a significant purpose is a key problem with many school teams. Putting together schedules, studying data, and doing work imposed from outside the team were cited as examples of the uninspiring kinds of tasks most teams worked on.

One team from Nebraska decided to create a vision worthy of their time by asking themselves, "What do we want our students to say about this team when they look back on their time with us?" They came up with things like: "They helped us develop a system for solving complex problems and taught us not to give up when work is hard" and "They made me fall in love with reading." These are the kinds of visions teams can dedicate themselves to and would be hard pressed to accomplish alone.

Daniel Pink, in his book *Drive* (2009), states that what motivates a team is a sense of purpose, autonomy, and competence. Pink has a clip on YouTube that can help you establish your vision (http://www.youtube.com/watch?v=AyRu7k70Jhc).

When you are ready to move forward on establishing a successful team, begin with this activity.

Activity: What's Our Sentence?

Purpose: Create an inspiring vision that results in both the enjoyment of teamwork as well as a sense of pride in the quality the team produces

Time: 30 minutes

Materials: Internet access, computer, projector, sticky notes, chart paper

Processing Tools: Brainstorming

Procedure:

1. Watch the Daniel Pink video.

2. Brainstorm words or phrases stating what the team will accomplish that will have a significant impact on students (see an excellent brainstorm protocol by viewing "Brainstorming Done Right" http://www.youtube.com/watch?v=9K8W4ooygUU).

3. Combine and consolidate your ideas into three or four powerful thoughts.

4. Divide your team into pairs. Each pair writes an inspiring vision sentence incorporating these thoughts.

5. Share the statements and combine the ideas to form a sentence that will drive your team's work.

Once your sentence is determined, ask these seven questions to verify that the sentence you selected is worth committing significant time and energy to.

A. Is this team's work something that is personally important to me?

B. Could I accomplish this just as effectively by myself?

C. Will this group and its work have a positive impact on my personal growth and that of my students?

D. Are the results worth the time and effort I am being asked to give?

E. Will my contributions be valued by this team?

F. Do I have or can I develop the skills needed to make a real contribution to this group's work?

G. "What differences will we see for our students and ourselves when our team creates this new reality?" and "Is this challenge big enough and important enough to keep us excited about working and growing together?"

If "no" is the answer to any of these questions, your team should revisit and revise the vision sentence. People must feel challenged by the work but not be overwhelmed by it. The best way to make the vision seem both challenging and doable is to involve all members in creating goals that will make this vision a reality. A worthy vision won't be a quick fix. It may guide your team's work for years.

Setting Goals

Writing challenging goals requires breaking the vision down into doable steps, laying out a realistic timeline, and agreeing up front about what constitutes high quality work. This activity can help you get started.

Activity: Vision to Reality

Purpose: Clarifying the vision by creating a step-by-step plan with assessments and benchmarks

Time: Two sessions of 40 minutes

Materials: Chart paper, sticky notes, markers, pens

Processing Tools: Brainstorming and affinity diagram

Procedure:

1. Study the vision sentence and ask each person to individually brainstorm goals for accomplishing this vision. Write one goal per sticky note.

2. Cluster goals either individually or as a group. Give each category a title. This focusing process is referred to as an "affinity diagram." For a video example of using affinity diagrams go to http://www.youtube.com/watch?v=f9sfJTp8tzc.

3. Divide the team into pairs. Ask each pair to map out suggested steps on a timeline for reaching the vision using the categories from the affinity diagram. This allows everyone's ideas to become clearer and the team can consider several implementation options.

4. Combine the ideas from the pairs and place the goals on a timeline.

5. Answer the questions, "How will we know if what we created works for students? What data will we collect to measure our successes or know when to make adjustments to the plan and how often will we collect it?" Add that information to the timeline as benchmarks.

6. Brainstorm ways to anticipate and address barriers along the way. Will you need training to build the skills for this? Who can help you if you get stuck? What resources will you need?

7. Check for clarity. Can everyone on the team now articulate the same compelling vision and the proposed action plan for getting there?

8. Post your sentence in the planning room and begin each meeting by stating the sentence and close each meeting

by asking, "Are we closer to this vision today than we were yesterday?"

Now that the "what, when, how, and why" questions are addressed, the next question is "who?" People want a clear understanding of how they fit into the team and what their personal roles and responsibilities will be.

Clarifying Roles and Responsibilities

Once people believe in the vision, they need to see that their input will be valued. Each person needs to play an active role in every meeting and feel the power of their contributions. If one person becomes too dominant or if members hold back, the team ceases to act like a team. On smaller teams people may assume multiple roles. Using the following role descriptions, members can choose the best fit and switch back and forth between assuming the role of captain or crew. This prevents anyone from becoming just cargo.

Coordinator. This person ensures that everyone understands the "who, what, when, where, and why" before the meetings. The coordinator organizes data and sends out timed agendas, meeting reminders, and other communications at least four days before the meeting. During the meeting, the coordinator leads decision-making discussions. The coordinator needs to be sensitive to group dynamics and able to go into action at the first sign of conflict or behavior that is inconsistent with team norms. The coordinator also makes certain conversations are balanced during every meeting. If a member is being particularly quiet the coordinator asks,

"So what are your thoughts at this point, Greg?" If a member is monopolizing the conversation, the coordinator might say, "Let me summarize your key points, Patty." This honors Patty's contribution before inviting another team member to talk.

Timekeeper. This member helps the team establish timetables for work and tries to anticipate and prevent delays. For example, if a discussion gets side-tracked or starts rehashing the same points, the timekeeper gives a gentle reminder like, "We have two more minutes allotted to this topic. Should we table this discussion for the next meeting or do you think we can do justice to it in the next two minutes?" This generally refocuses the conversation and moves it forward. If a housekeeping task like planning a fieldtrip is coming up, the timekeeper asks for suggestions via e-mail or puts together a subcommittee to get some of the legwork completed in advance. This prevents minor tasks from taking up important collaboration time during meetings. An efficient rule is "never use the whole team to do what can be handled by fewer people."

Analyzer. The analyzer is the critical friend who gently calls attention to potential flaws or weaknesses in team plans or processes. This person insists that potential problems be addressed before they become barriers to the work. This can sound like, "You know, this sounds like a great plan for us but what effect do you think this change will have on the other departments?" or "What prerequisite skills should we consider for students who are not ready for this material?" Taking the perspective of other stakeholders before implementation prevents reworking later. The analyzer also leads discussions for coming up with constructive solutions for these potential problems.

Recorder. The recorder keeps detailed notes of all participants, key decisions, action plans, and assignments. These notes should be completed using a consistent format and should be distributed within 24 hours. This provides members with documentation of their assignments and commitments. Typing minutes on a computer and projecting them on a screen enables the recorder to push "send" at the end of the meeting and complete this job easily.

Summarizer. The summarizer listens for opportunities to recap what has been said in order to facilitate and clarify discussions. If a conversation starts to go over the same points, go off topic, or becomes complicated, a quick review of goals, points of agreement, and what still needs to be accomplished can put the group back on track. It may sound as simple as, "Ok, let me go over two points where we have agreement so far. . . . Now the only point that still needs to be clarified is. . . right?" The summarizer also goes over key points at the end of the meeting to give the group a chance to review their progress and make certain nothing major has been omitted from the minutes.

Activity: Who Does What
Purpose: Agree upon role descriptions and assignments
Time: 10–15 minutes
Materials: Copies of role descriptions
Processing Tools: None

Procedure:

1. Discuss the suggested role descriptions and adjust or combine them to fit your own team. Should some of the descriptions be explained in more detail? Should any of them be subdivided or combined?

2. Now have each person rank the roles in order of "most comfortable to least comfortable for me" and share this information with the group.

3. Based upon this feedback decide how to assign roles and for how long.

This activity avoids putting people in the awkward position of not feeling competent in their assigned roles. It also prevents one member from snapping up and hanging on to a role that three people would enjoy trying. Some teams use a monthly sign-up sheet to decide which roles members will assume at various meetings.

Once your team has agreed on roles and responsibilities they need to establish a structure for their meeting time.

Establishing Norms

Norms are belief statements that guide the team members' interactions and behaviors. Norms need to be short, simple statements. These codes of behavior support both quality work and each member's rights and ideas.

Consider these issues when setting norms.

1. Meeting time (beginning, ending, frequency and lengths of meetings, agendas)

Sample norm: We will arrive on time, follow the agenda, and end on time.

2. Communication protocols (pausing, paraphrasing, asking probing questions, assuming positive intentions, interrupting, sending reminders and updates)

Sample norm: All team members are equal and will be thoughtfully listened to.

3. Confidentiality

Sample norm: Concerns about the team will be discussed within the team before going outside the team.

4. Decision making (what processes to use for decisions, how work is to be assigned, rubrics for quality work, how to resolve conflicts of opinions or schedule)

Sample norm: We will make decisions by consensus with majority rules as our backup process.

5. Everyone has equal voice (monopolizing, being passive, using strategies like clock partners, numbered heads, paired reading, holding each other accountable)

Sample norms: Leadership will rotate based upon the type of meeting. If you commit to something, do it in a timely manner.

Teams without norms leave themselves open to potential relationship problems and misunderstandings. Here is one way to establish norms:

Activity: Rules to Live By
Purpose: Establish norms that will increase productivity and facilitate team goals
Time: 1 hour

Materials: Sticky note, chart paper, markers
Processing Tools: Brainstorm and affinity diagram
Procedure:

1. Make certain all members are present for this exercise.

2. Without talking, brainstorm five or six ideal behaviors for an effective team. Put each idea on a separate sticky note.

3. The coordinator collects all sticky notes and clusters like ideas, providing as much anonymity as possible. Each set of ideas is read aloud, discussed, and moved to a different cluster if needed.

4. The team then creates a norm statement for each cluster.

5. Ask each member to identify any norm they cannot commit to. Openly discuss what changes can be made to a norm that does not have universal support.

6. Record agreed-upon norms on a poster.

Norms are reviewed at the beginning of every meeting by the coordinator and quickly evaluated at the end of the meeting by the summarizer. Norms can be expanded or revised as necessary. Norms should always be revisited when a new member joins the team.

High performing teams not only follow norms but also agree to confront behaviors that violate them. Many teams we interviewed identified low trust as the primary reason for people avoiding addressing violations. This eventually throws teams into dysfunction and malcontent.

Once you have this framework the team will spend more time on work and less time on resolving interpersonal problems. Now it's time to put protocols for productive meetings in place.

Establishing Meeting Protocols

Getting Started. A team of teachers from California said that they raised their meeting productivity by using a simple activity called "Jeers and Cheers." They started each meeting by focusing on feelings, views, and opinions of members. This short but powerful strategy generated a friendly atmosphere where people built relationships through quick personal discussions. Here is their strategy.

Activity: Jeers and Cheers
Purpose: Build rapport and create positive energy
Time: 3 minutes for both parts of the activity
Materials: None
Processing Tools: None
Procedure:

1. The first minute of every meeting is about "moans and groans." Anything you feel like complaining about is fair game as long as it is not an attack on any person. Complain about the workload, how the students are behaving, or that you didn't get your bathroom break. This is all fair game. Confessing the sins of bosses and others is not. Once you've stated your issue you have to let it go and get to the real work of the team. The entire team has to fit all complaints into the same 60 seconds either by talking to a partner or using round robin for the group. Team members always have the option to pass.

2. During the next two minutes, members share something about themselves (feelings, values, accomplishments, and interests) without any fear of judgment. Someone poses a sentence starter like, "Tell us something you accomplished this week that you are proud of" or "Tell your partner one thing we could do to improve our team meetings." This can be a round-robin discussion where everyone makes a one-sentence statement for the entire team to hear, or partners can exchange information. This strategy works best when people know the question or prompt ahead of time.

Every problem you tackle and every decision you make either builds or detracts from team trust and relationships. Steven Covey says relationships between people are like "emotional bank accounts" where we constantly make deposits and withdrawals (1989). Covey describes clear expectations, small kindnesses, listening, and following through on commitments as actions that "make deposits" in emotional accounts. Conversely, things like disrespect, interrupting, ignoring, and letting people down become "withdrawals." To make a team function well we have to intentionally make daily deposits in each other's emotional accounts and remember to apologize when we make withdrawals. This is the stuff of great families, friendships, and high-performing teams.

Timelines. Agreeing that all team members will complete assignments on time is an important norm to set. Delaying the team's work by not following through on commitments in a timely fashion is one of the "team killing" issues, according to many groups we interviewed. Ken Blanchard's research of 2,044 team leaders found that 44 percent cited "individuals who do not complete assignments" as one of the most frustrating things about being part of a team (2006).

Teams must keep in mind that members have other commitments running alongside of their team project work that has to be factored into timelines. If your group has little experience estimating the type of large project you are about to work on, consider using a tool called PERT (Project Evaluation and Review Technique), often applied in business settings (Gingrich, 2014).

Simply stated, this formula uses three estimates: the most likely amount of time required (Tm), the most optimistic amount of time (To) and the most pessimistic amount of time required (Tp). To come up with the estimates for your task or project simply add: 4Tm + To + Tp and divide this by 6. You now have a reasonable estimate for the amount of time this work will take.

Try applying this formula to one of the projects your team is tackling. Did you find this tool helpful?

Timed Agendas. When Margaret served on a state administrator's board, the meetings went on for hours, often because of time spent rehashing the same issues and arguments. Finally, the director came up with a technique that cut the meeting time in half. The major change was simply dividing the main agenda into two main parts: "items for discussion" and "items for action." Here are the guidelines:

Things listed under "Items for discussion" are never decided upon during that meeting. The group only explores pros, cons, and possibilities. These discussion items are then placed in the "items for action" for the following meeting.

"Items for action" are briefly reviewed by summarizing the pros and cons from the prior meeting. No rehashing of old points is allowed. Only new issues about this item are entertained for discussion. This moves decision making along because people have ample time between meetings to do extra research, talk, and think about the issues before making their commitment. This procedure makes timed agendas easier to manage.

Timed agendas work efficiently because each agenda item has a maximum time assigned to it. Because the time-keeper insists that the group move the discussion to the next item when time is up, people stop admiring problems and get to the business of solving them. Expect that deciding how many minutes to assign each item will be difficult at first, but once the procedure is used for several meetings the payoff will more than offset the initial frustrations.

Follow through is more likely when people have a clear idea of both agendas and timelines. Good preparation is dependent upon the coordinator's ability to give members lead time to reflect and in some cases get together with sub-groups to plan their part of the work. Forwarding material and reminders using short e-mails, screencasts, or video clips is an efficient practice. The short and to-the-point e-mail might look like Figure 1.

FIGURE 1: Team Agenda Example

Team Vision: We will make it possible for each student to exceed expectations.

Next team meeting: Wednesday, October 15 at 7:30 AM in the Team Room

Purpose: Increasing students' abilities to justify inferences.

Item	Specifics	Who	How	Time
Opening exercise		Tia	See "Cheers and Jeers" activity	3 min.
Norms and vision		Morgan	Quick review	1 min.
Items for discussion	What tools and strategies can we use to teach students to draw inferences?		Brainstorming	7 min.

	Which tools will work for kids who need pre-requisite skills? Advanced skills?		Affinity diagram for 5 levels of difficulty	12 min.
Items for action	Final approval for December's authentic assessment and rubric for social studies/literacy	Juan	Review and approve	4 min.
Reflection	Recap of key points and how did our meeting go?	Bev	See "Plus Delta" activity	4 min.
Next agenda	What will be our goal and tasks for the next meeting? How will this affect our vision?	Morgan	Review "Issue Bin" ideas & next steps	3 min.

The only way for teams to get better at managing their time is to allow time at the end of meetings to reflect on the team's efficiency. Here are two quick procedures that will help.

Activity: Strengths and Concerns
Purpose: To solicit feedback at the end of a meeting, end of a week, or end of a project
Time: 3–4 minutes
Materials: Chart paper or dry erase board, markers
Process Tools: Plus Delta
Procedure:

1. Draw a T chart on large piece of chart paper, blackboard, or dry erase board.

2. Write + (symbolizes the strengths) on one side of the chart and Δ (to symbolize the need for change) on the other side of the chart.

3. Establish the ground rule that one person speaks at a time.

4. The coordinator asks team members to list the strengths of the meeting or project and writes them on the + side of the chart.

5. The coordinator then asks the team, "What could have been done better or improved?" and writes those statements on the Δ side of the chart.

6. A third column can be added for brainstorming ideas for improvement.

For a video model of the "Plus Delta" process go to http://
www.youtube.com/watch?v=ADEd0IIswpQ.

Activity: Parking Lot
Purpose: Capture ideas, questions, or concerns
Time: Ongoing process tool
Materials: Chart paper, sticky notes
Process Tools: Issue bin
Procedure:

1. Using a large sheet of paper, write ISSUE BIN or
PARKING LOT at the top.

2. Post in meeting room to capture ideas, questions,
or concerns that are off topic but need to be addressed at
a later time.

3. At the end of the meeting decide how and when to
address any items on this paper.

The strongest teams know that accomplishing work is
directly dependent upon building and maintaining relationships. By setting up and following the guidelines and
protocols in this section, every voice is heard and ideas are
honored. These small but consistent drops of "team oil"
reduce friction and make repeated deposits in each team
member's emotional bank account. Later, when teammates
make emotional withdrawals, they will have a sense of
belonging and trust that will not break the team's emotional
bank—and there will be emotional withdrawals.

Managing and Resolving Conflict

If two men on the same job agree all the time, then one is use-less. If they disagree all the time, both are useless.

—Darryl F. Zanuck

The Storming Stage of Teaming

As the honeymoon period closes, problems invariably start to surface. People begin to realize that working as a team is more taxing and complex than it originally sounded. People begin to question people's motives and goals. They begin to disagree over what final products should look like or become dissatisfied with how much time the work is taking. At this stage it is normal for people to experience a loss of enthusiasm for teamwork. They worry about what they have gotten themselves into.

Relationships among members is the most volatile component of teamwork at this point. When people feel under-appreciated, disrespected, or left out they experience "burn out" and want to disengage. Feelings of dissatisfaction result in wallowing in unproductive griping and arguing behaviors unless someone recognizes that listening to and supporting each other is the way to move beyond this lull in productivity.

What Does the Team Need at This Stage?

This is the point where the group must focus on their vision as they learn to handle disagreements without becoming disagreeable or judgmental. They need to learn from mistakes, forget, forgive, and move on. This is the time to reexamine how well roles, norms, and communication skills are being implemented.

If you sense a lack of commitment to the work of the team, the factors described in Figure 2 (Villa & Thousand, 1995) will help you analyze where your system may be breaking down. An unclear vision results in confusion, whereas insufficient skill to accomplish the vision causes people to feel anxious. When the incentive or payoff is not perceived as worth the effort, passive response or active resistance is likely to result. If the team cannot access needed resources, frustration sets in and if the team doesn't have consensus on clear action steps, anything from a series of false starts to total abandonment of the vision is likely.

Take a look at Figure 2 and see which factors may be the source of your team's difficulty. Have your vision and norms been guiding your work? Are you still using the tools from the first section? If the answer is yes then perhaps communication and conflict management will be the next things to look at.

Building trust and maintaining trust will be the key to team success. What does this imply? Trust is the intersection between being trusting and trustworthy. It takes both qualities on the part of all team members to create a high performing team. Try the next activity and see where your team is strong and where there is a need for attention.

FIGURE 2 Chart For Managing Complex Change

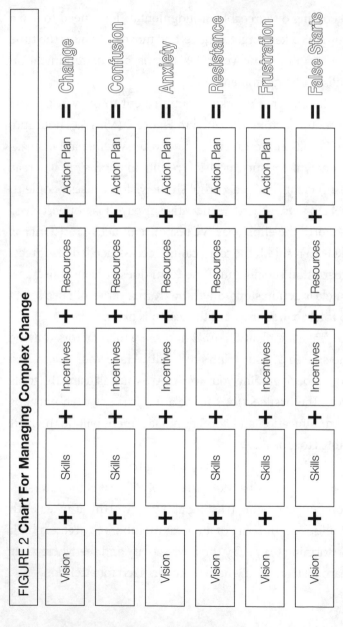

Vision	+	Skills	+	Incentives	+	Resources	+	Action Plan	=	Change
	+	Skills	+	Incentives	+	Resources	+	Action Plan	=	Confusion
Vision	+		+	Incentives	+	Resources	+	Action Plan	=	Anxiety
Vision	+	Skills	+		+	Resources	+	Action Plan	=	Resistance
Vision	+	Skills	+	Incentives	+		+	Action Plan	=	Frustration
Vision	+	Skills	+	Incentives	+	Resources	+		=	False Starts

Adapted from *Creating an Inclusive School* (p. 58) by R. Villa and J. Thousand, 1995.

Activity: How strong is our trust?

Purpose: To talk about trust in concrete terms so the team can pinpoint areas for growth and celebrate their strengths

Time: 10 minutes

Materials: Venn Diagram

Process Tools: None

Procedure:

1. Each person receives a Venn diagram. Ask them to visualize the most trustworthy person they know—someone they would trust their child or their life with. Have them silently write specific traits of that trustworthy person in the left circle of the Venn.

2. Share and compile the master list with the group. Traits like competent, honest, dependable, good listener, and uses good judgment will start this description.

3. Now silently make a list of traits that describe a trusting person. This is the person you must become when you turn your child or part of your life over to someone you trust. Share this list with the group. Now you will see things like open, forgiving, willing to take a risk, willing to learn, and see both sides of an argument as the key traits.

4. Have a discussion about which is more difficult and what type of environment it will take to help your team members be both trustworthy and trusting.

There are five key areas for reducing conflict and increasing trust: listening, avoiding blame, giving honest feedback, staying within your circle of influence, and conflict resolution.

Effective Listening

Dale Carnegie talks about three types of listening: selective, attentive, or proactive. Selective listening happens when we choose to ignore the other person by allowing ourselves to be preoccupied with what we want to say. Attentive listening happens when you give full attention to the facts and feelings being communicated. Proactive listening happens when you are not only attentive but also ask elaborative questions and elaborate on the other person's ideas.

Activity: How well do we listen?

Purpose: Analyze the levels of listening typical of your meetings and create a plan for growth

Time: 3–10 minutes

Materials: YouTube video, chart paper

Process Tools: Consensogram

Procedure:

1. Prepare a consensogram chart for listening. Across the top of the chart put the words: selective, attentive, and proactive. Draw a Likert scale ranging from 1–9 across the bottom of the chart to guide the rating process.

Selective	Attentive	Proactive
1 2 3	4 5 6	7 8 9

2. View the video "Effective Listening and Communication Skills: Dale Carnegie Training" http://www.youtube.com/

watch?v=cPjED3teZ7E. Under each listening category list the traits you remember from the video. This will be your rubric.

3. On a slip of paper, privately rate the team on how well you feel they listen to you on a scale of 1–9. For example, if I believe my team listens pretty well I will rate them 4 under attentive listening. Hand this paper to your analyzer who will then post everyone's rating for listening.

4. What patterns do you see? What opportunities for improvement can you suggest?

One way to improve is to use paraphrasing. It is tempting to make assumptions when you don't have enough information or you have a preconceived notion. Paraphrasing is a tool that helps members check perceptions in order to reduce assumptions that result in misunderstandings.

Simply restating what a person said is not paraphrasing. Paraphrasing is putting what you think the other person meant into your own words. For example, if John frowns and says, "This is going to be a whale of a lot of work," your paraphrase might be, "So you don't think the team should take this project on?" This gives John the opportunity to confirm that that is exactly what he meant or clarify that he is all for the project but in view of the level of challenge, he thinks the deadline is too aggressive.

Here are some lead-in phrases that will help with paraphrasing:

- Let me see if I get what you are saying. Basically you want to. . .

- I get the impression that you mean. . .
- Basically you feel that. . .
- Do you mean that. . .?

We are always guessing what other people are thinking to some extent. If done correctly, paraphrasing not only increases proactive listening but also catches and corrects misconceptions, false assumptions, and errors.

If paraphrasing is a way to make a difficult situation better, then blaming would be the way to make things worse.

Blaming

In the storming stage, people often try to pin responsibility on someone else when things go wrong. This damages trust levels by causing feelings of resentment and stress. In the book *The Wisdom of Oz*, Connors and Smith say blaming or finger pointing puts people into a victim cycle (2014). There is no room for shaming (I can't believe you did that) or blaming (because of you…) in productive team work. When things go wrong it doesn't matter whose fault it is. What matters is how we choose to respond to disappointment and adversity.

Instead of reacting like victims, successful teams ask themselves how they can proactively address the difficult situation. They take charge of problem situations by analyzing the problem, owning it, finding a solution, and taking action. They live by the norm "Tackle issues, not each other."

Most conflicts result from errors or misunderstandings that are co-created. The most helpful response is to acknowledge how you may have contributed to the problem and then ask for help solving it. For example, "Greg, I'm sorry, I may not have been clear about when I needed that material, so now we need to figure out how we are going to get this report done by Tuesday." Notice how there is no mention of the other person's contribution to the problem. Even if you do not believe you are the main culprit, it helps to follow this model.

Giving honest and productive feedback is another communication skill that reduces stress and increases trust. Your colleagues deserve feedback on the effects they are having on you, both positive and negative. Telling them when they inspire you or make you feel supported is easy, but being honest about the other side of the coin is more difficult.

Honest Feedback

Never choose to be miserable because of a teammate's poor behavior and remember that people cannot correct problems they are unaware of. Have a private conversation to let people know where they stand, in a way that neither blames nor judges. "Bob, your bad attitude is ruining our meetings" is judgmental, vague, and blaming. Effective feedback will sound like, "Bob, I noticed that you and Ellen are crossing your arms and having a lot of sidebar conversations during meetings. It makes me wonder if there are problems you are reluctant to bring up in front of the group." The latter statement is clear, specific, descriptive, and nonjudgmental. This approach addresses the issue while making this difficult message easier to deal with.

Activity: Reframing feedback
Purpose: To practice ways of giving clear, specific, and non-judgmental feedback in difficult situations
Time: 15 minutes
Materials: Chart paper and markers
Process Tools: None
Procedure:

1. Set up a chart using a variety of harsh statements that could come up within teams.

2. Decide what makes these statements seem counterproductive.

3. Restate them in a way that addresses the problem without damaging relationships.

Poorly phrased	Why this is a poor example	Create a good feedback statement
You talk too much.		
You have a bad attitude.		
You procrastinate.		

As the receiver of this information, you do not have to agree with the feedback but it is helpful when you acknowledge the points made, ask for clarification, acknowledge points you agree with, and show that you at least understand points you do not agree with. For example, "So you are saying that I need to address my questions to the team instead of just to Ellen. Is that right?

Clear feedback statements give people an opportunity to explain their behavior or apologize for what is currently viewed as poor conduct on their part. Make certain you invite people to give you feedback on how your behavior is affecting them as well. Taking responsibility for mistakes by apologizing and changing your behavior as a result of these conversations shows deep respect and builds trust.

It is not helpful to let things over which you or your team have no control interfere with things you can do something about. The prevailing wisdom is to stay within your circle of influence to avoid feelings of helplessness.

Circle of Influence

Steven Covey describes "your circle of influence" as things over which you have control or can influence (1989). For example, we cannot force people to change, so we have two choices. We can waste time sitting around worrying or whining about how horrible things are or we can ask ourselves what we can do about the situation.

Teams that spend a lot of time discussing things they can do absolutely nothing about need to let those conversations go. Valid or not, focusing outside our circle of influence leads to feelings of being helpless and results in precious team time wasted.

Some teams monitor this "helpless/hopeless" language in a light-hearted way by passing an object like a rubber chicken to members using unproductive talk. The only way to get rid of the chicken is to catch another team member making the same error. Self-monitoring increases awareness of bad habits and awareness empowers us to take corrective action.

Conflict Resolution

You cannot control your feelings, but you do choose how you react to those feelings. When tough issues and conflicts arise, the way you choose to communicate influences the team culture. Here are a few guidelines, based on Barbara Sanderson's work, for managing the team conflicts that inevitably occur in all teams sooner or later (2005).

When disagreements occur:

1. Initiate a problem-solving conversation within a week.

2. Avoid all shaming and blaming during these conversations.

3. Go directly to the person(s) before telling or involving any third party.

4. Do not become the third party in anyone else's conflict.

5. Be open to both positive and negative feedback.

6. Remain open to adjusting your expectations.

7. Be ready to come up with several solutions for every problem that surfaces.

If you feel the need to vent to other people about your conflict, it means that it is past time to have that one-to-one conversation directly with the person involved. Going to someone else will only make the problem worse for you and your team's working relationships. Also keep in mind that changing the other person is not a good expectation. Stay within your circle of influence and remember that the only person you can change is yourself. Be open to working through frustrations and confusion.

During these tough conversations remember to:

1. Invite the person to solve the problem with you.

2. Talk in a private place where you will not be interrupted.

3. Briefly define what is happening and the effect it is having on you or on the group and ask if that matches the other person's perception. Listen intently. The more specific you are about the problem the less room there is for miscommunication.

4. Identify the exact areas of agreement and disagreement.

5. Acknowledge your own part in creating this situation but don't go on and on about it.

6. Identify what each of you need to feel satisfied with the results.

7. Don't stifle or dwell on anger or frustration.

8. Clarify what each person's commitment is to resolving the situation and lay out a clear step-by-step action plan.

Mirroring without distorting the other person's message is important. The following activity is especially helpful for opening communication when people have very different ideas on how to solve a problem.

Activity: Another Person's Shoes
Purpose: To resolve conflict by seeing things from another person's point of view
Time: 10–15 minutes
Materials: Talking stick
Process Tools: Talking stick
Procedure:

1. Start by choosing a topic where there are two opposing points of view. For example, "How should we solve the problem of student apathy?" or "How important are common assessments for our team?"

2. Divide the team into pairs who are willing to debate the issue from two different points of view.

3. Partner A presents his or her point of view for one to two minutes while partner B listens carefully. Partner B then presents while partner A listens.

4. Each partner then assumes the other person's position and debates the subject from the opposing point of view.

5. After the debate, the team discusses what they learned from the exercise. What insights did you have? What surprised you? How can we apply these insights in our meetings?

What if This Doesn't Work?

Sometimes communication breaks down or your timing may not be right when problem-solving conversations occur.

Reflect on your own role and check to see how you could have been clearer or less judgmental during the conversation. How well did you listen and accept the other person's point of view?

When conflicts continue, you basically have three good choices that will not destroy trust, none of which involve complaining to outsiders. You may choose to go back to the team and try having the discussion using a different approach. You may decide that involving a neutral party to facilitate the conversation would help, or you might just decide to drop it and live with the situation without feeling resentful or complaining.

If your team has resolved the confusion and disillusionment of the early stages of teaming they have weathered enough storms together and built enough trust to start working harmoniously. If so, you are now entering the Norming stage of teaming.

Refining Decision-Making Skills

Decision is a sharp knife that cuts clean and straight: indecision, a dull one that hacks and tears and leaves ragged edges behind.

—Gordon Graham

The Norming Stage of Teaming

In the Norming stage there is renewed energy for teamwork. Collaboration and productivity leaps forward because people are willing to put aside individual wants for the good of the team. The group is sick and tired of arguing and has resolved some major differences so they are less likely to recruit people to "take their side," but they may still be reluctant to bring up anything that would throw the team back into the fight-flight stage of storming.

What the Team Needs At This Stage

Because side-stepping controversial issues and avoiding discussing sticky problems is a sure-fire way to throw the team back into the stage they think they are avoiding, the group now needs to learn to intentionally create win-win situations. They need to refine their decision-making protocols and build enough trust to have open and honest conversations that avoid the tensions caused by unresolved issues.

Creating Win-Win Situations

To maintain a win-win environment, people need to step back and let another person get what he or she needs or wants first. If it is about you winning at the expense of another person you are not a good team player.

Activity: I'm the Winner

Purpose: To demonstrate win-win thinking

Time: 3 minutes

Materials: None

Procedure:

1. Each person selects a partner and stands face-to-face and hand-to-hand.

2. Everyone listens carefully before moving. Say, "Your task is to keep your hands in full contact with each other as you get your partner to take two steps backward. Ready? Go."

3. Stop after one minute. You generally see one of two things happen. Either both partners stand there pushing on each other's hands and no one goes anywhere, or one partner overpowers or tricks the other into moving. This models the kind of win/lose relationship that results in a withdrawal on the loser's emotional bank account—not a good practice for building high functioning teams.

4. Now demonstrate the option they may not have considered. Stand hand to hand with your partner and say, "We both need to get the other person to move backward, right? Do you want me to go backward first or will you move first? You see, both of us accomplish the goal with no pushing, shoving, bullying, or losers."

5. Now ask the team to debrief the point of this demonstration. What does win-win look like in a team meeting when it isn't a game? Give examples.

You have to agree on exactly what win/win is or you won't know if you have it. Both people have to create a situation where there is mutual benefit.

Problem Behaviors

A school in Toledo, Ohio had a problem with several teachers habitually showing up at least five minutes late for meetings. Because the team waited for these members to arrive, more and more teachers began coming later and later. To address this problem they created a new norm, saying, "Even if people are missing we start on time." Most people responded by showing up promptly and appreciated the fact that their time was now being respected. They also agreed that absent members or late arrivers would be responsible for catching up after, not during, the meeting. It was amazing how much this small adjustment in thinking improved both team effectiveness and overall attitude about teamwork.

Remember to do the "plus delta" activity at the close of each meeting even though you have reached the norming phase of teaming. This allows the group to address issues early enough to prevent bigger problems with morale and inefficient work patterns later.

Time Between Meetings

Maintaining win-win requires clear and consistent communication and procedures that prevent problem behaviors from eating away at morale. Stand-up meetings and the talking stick strategies are two powerful ways to promote trust through healthy communication.

Activity: Stand-up Meetings
Purpose: Personal accountability, quick communication, and team support between meetings

Time: 5–10 minutes
Materials: Coin, pen, and paper
Procedure:

- Stand up meetings are typically five to ten minutes in length and are used as daily check-ins to keep communication current and supportive. All members stand in a circle and pass a coin as they answer three questions as briefly as possible. What have I accomplished? What will I do today? Is there any help I need? No problem-solving conversations are held during this meeting but team members can respond with congratulations or needed assistance later in the day

The talking stick procedure makes certain that good listening is happening. The results are amazing. Speakers become clearer and listeners become more focused on what is being said.

Activity: Talking stick
Purpose: Healing or promoting positive relationships through a climate of listening
Time: Varies with conversation
Materials: Talking stick or pencil
Process Tools: Talking stick
Procedure:

1. Person A is given the talking stick and is the only person allowed to talk for one minute.

2. Person A then hands the talking stick to person B, who must repeat what person A said.

3. The rule is that no one may make a new point until they can restate the other person's point to their satisfaction. See the Steven Covey site http://www.youtube.com/watch?v=HUxi-Zc45tA for more information about talking sticks.

4. How might you integrate this listening procedure into your team meetings?

Listening is a critical skill for keeping trust levels high, and clarifying how team decisions will be made is another key area.

Decision-Making Options

One way to establish win-win is to match your decision-making process to the situation. All team members must know exactly what part they will have in each team decision. Here are several decision-making protocols to choose from. Each has pros and cons.

1. **Leader Decides.** The leader makes the decision with little or no input from the team. This quick and simple process works well for minor decisions where the team has little desire to give input and trusts the leader to make good choices. Be careful though—lack of involvement causes people not to remember much about these decisions except when they go south, and then it is tempting to blame the leader.

2. **Majority Rules.** After discussion, the team votes to settle differences of opinion. In this option the team feels included, it is fast, and generally works well for minor issues

where people aren't heavily invested in which way the vote goes. Because this process results in winners and losers, some members may feel little to no commitment to the decision. This option rarely works for important issues.

3. **Consensus.** Every member of the group agrees to support the decision to some extent. This process takes more time, but people feel more committed in the end. Conflict is a natural part of consensus and people may try to put pressure on each other.

Consensus does not necessarily mean everyone gets their own way or is even totally satisfied in the end. It is a way to arrive at a decision every member can support. One consensus process is called the "Fist-to-Five."

Fist-to-Five

In fist-to-five, a potential decision is put on the table. After each person has the opportunity to present their ideas, pros, cons, and points of view, someone asks for a show of fingers to indicate the level of acceptance and support for the decision as read or amended.

- Five fingers up means full support. I am willing to take a leadership role.
- Four fingers up is full support. I will assist in leading this effort and support others.
- Three fingers up is full support. I will implement enthusiastically.

- Two fingers up is full support with some hesitation. I will implement until the designated review period at which time I may continue or withdraw my support.
- One finger up is I am unsure of this decision and choose not to implement at this time. I actively support those who do implement and will do nothing to sabotage this effort.
- A fist means there is something about this decision that prevents me from supporting it. The fist stops the consensus process because there is not universal support. Discussions must continue until the plan can be modified enough to reach consensus or a backup decision-making method should be used.

It is wise to ask the dissenting member to identify what parts of the decision he or she does agree with and what would have to change to make the decision acceptable. Often the changes improve the decision and the dissenting member moves from a fist to high support.

A tool called Nominal Group Technique helps ensure that all members have had a say in making the decision. Decisions also tend to be of better quality when this technique is employed.

Activity: Cast your Votes

Purpose: Provide everyone on the team an equal voice in decision making

Time: 25 minutes

Materials: Chart paper, markers, colored dots

Processing Tools: Nominal group technique

Procedure:

1. Brainstorm ideas for solving a team problem and cluster ideas into categories on chart paper.

2. Establish clear criteria for choosing the most important items on the list (e.g., within our circle of influence, can be implemented immediately, has principal support, within the budget).

3. Each person is given two dots of different colors. The red dot is the team member's first choice and is worth one vote. A green dot represents their second choice and is worth half a vote. Dots are privately placed next to each team member's choices.

4. Dot values are totaled up and the score placed next to each option.

5. The results of the vote are discussed openly, allowing the group to make decisions based upon the results. This can reveal some inconsistencies and an opportunity for reconsideration.

Which processes a team uses depends upon several factors. Here are some guidelines to help select and implement any of the protocols.

1. How important is this decision?

2. Which people need to be involved in this decision and why?

3. Which kind of input is needed from each member?

4. What is our time limit for the process?

5. What fallback process will we use if the first decision-making strategy does not work out?

No matter how good a decision is, the proof is in the results. You need to "inspect what you expect" or someone is likely to drop the ball along the way.

Evaluate and Celebrate Successes

The more a team self-assesses and tracks its own progress, the more likely it is that members will perform well and follow through. Accountability done well boosts productivity. Team members must feel responsible to one another but this cannot be a "got you" kind of accountability where people feel that they must defend and justify their actions. The team attitude has to be one of fixing problems and celebrating small successes, not judging each other. To foster this positive way of assessing, think about these guidelines:

1. The purpose of the work, the standards for excellence of the end product, and individual roles and responsibilities must be very clear.

2. The entire team must have a hand in developing and refining the standards.

3. People must be given freedom to meet these standards in their own way.

4. The team must meet regularly to track and analyze their own performance.

5. Performance feedback must be used to solve problems as soon as possible.

To develop a culture of accountability people must feel free to openly own up to mistakes without fear of being judged or punished. Errors need to be looked upon as opportunities for learning and repetitive mistakes call for immediate preventive action. One school in Nebraska started each meeting by bringing up the "blunder of the week." The team took a few minutes to solve the problem or at least learn a "what not to do" lesson from the error discussed. This practice proved to be one of their best strategies for building trust and developing a culture of continuous improvement.

Once the team's culture is action-oriented and morale is strong, there is still room for improvement. Great teams know they don't have to be sick to get better and they get better by building individual and team capacity.

Building Team Capacity

You can never build a structure by just piling up the bricks... all available resources have to be put to use properly.

—Ram Mohan

The Performing Stage of Teaming

At the Performing stage, the glue of unity enables members to see dissent and differing opinions as a tool that improves quality. The oil of routines and procedures keeps things running smoothly and the group self-assesses regularly in their effort to improve. The unfortunate news is that these teams will revert to earlier stages of team development when there are changes in membership or when they take on projects that present significantly different challenges.

What Does the Team Need At This Stage?

Strong bonds of trust and efficiency now enable the team to switch their energy to building new skills. They no longer allow their time to be monopolized by simply reacting to the day-to-day stresses and demands. They think proactively, and improving capacity for problem solving becomes part of the team's regular work. One approach for building new skills and understandings is establishing an expert pool.

Expert Pool

An "expert pool" is an intentional, coordinated effort to strengthen performance and skill by developing experts within the team. The more skillful and capable team members become, the less time is wasted on plans that are ineffective. Here are the steps for building a pool of experts.

1. Brainstorm a list of student problems your team needs to solve. For example: reading comprehension, low motivation, poor memory skills, poor strategies for math word problems, disruptive behavior, and incomplete assignments.

2. Each member selects one of the areas to focus on for the year. People may want to work in pairs or as individuals.

3. Each quarter, every team member agrees to find and pilot at least one promising, research-based intervention that adds to their repertoire of solutions for the topic they

selected. They fine-tune their use of this intervention and then teach it to the rest of the team.

4. Develop an electronic database of new interventions and share them with other teams in the building.

By having each teacher find, implement, and share four new interventions a year, a team of five teachers can expand their expertise by 20 strategies. This embedded professional development targets the exact needs of the team and results in skillful members with quicker fixes. This practice has a huge impact on student learning.

Teaching other team members new strategies is risky business in some schools where there is low trust and people's motives are constantly questioned. The "who made you so smart" attitude can discourage talented teachers with a lot to share from stepping forward. Expert pools make this a normal way of doing business for everyone and thus creates a safe learning environment.

One way to raise the level of trust is to help team members understand that each person has a style of approaching work that may or may not be similar to their own. These differences in styles are often at the core of misunderstandings.

Understanding Styles

People tend to fall into four basic styles of working and communicating. Let's call the four major styles squares, circles, triangles, and squiggles. Although people relate to some aspects of every style, when put into a forced choice situation, one or two styles tend to be a natural fit.

Every style makes important contributions to the team's work and no style is more desirable than any of the others. Each style can tick off any of the others by being insensitive to their different priorities and ways of thinking. For example, what you see as firmness in yourself may be viewed as stubbornness by others. Knowledge of what each style values, what they appreciate, and what drives them nuts helps members understand their own as well as each other's reasoning. This makes team cooperation much easier to achieve.

A four corners technique allows people to self-select an area of the room that represents a choice or position they relate to and then engage in a discussion to support or clarify their choice. Here is an example of how to apply this technique to a discussion about personal styles.

Activity: What's Your Style?

Purpose: Build trust and respect by understanding people's differences in values, priorities, and styles of working

Time: 20 minutes

Materials: Description of the styles, picture of a square, circle, triangle, and squiggle, chart paper, and markers

Processing Tools: Four Corners

Procedure:

1. Place a picture of one shape in each corner of the room. Without hearing any description of the shapes, have people choose the shape in the corner of the room that best describes their style.

2. Read the descriptions aloud and tell people that they may change corners if they do not believe the description fits them well.

A. Squares are task-oriented. They value routines, procedures, organization, attention to detail, and productivity. They take notes and make timelines even when they are not required to do so. They prefer to work alone but bring structure and organization to a team. What drives squares nuts are unclear directions, spontaneous changes in direction, inconsistency, and conflict. Squares sometimes have a tendency to get too detailed, to resist change, and to not think out of the box enough for other team members' liking.

B. Circles thrive on relationships and communication. They value cooperation, sincere effort, and the fun of working in groups. They are the first people to detect any breakdowns in communication or relationships and they spring into action to mend fences and draw people into activities. Circles appreciate a free flow of ideas, time to socialize, and practical applications of plans. Conflict, intense competition, work that is too detailed, and rigidity drives circles nuts. Circles can be disorganized, go off task, have sidebar conversations, forget deadlines, and be lax on follow-through.

C. Triangles are task-oriented and value quality results. Even though they generally prefer to work alone, they make good leaders because they set clear goals, are very organized, are careful analyzers, and ask "why, how long, how much, and how well" questions. They want accountability. They are not afraid of a challenge and tend to speak their mind. Sloppy work, being told what to do, goofing around in meetings, and lack of follow-through drives them nuts. Triangles can be confrontational, take over too much, and nit-pick on points of quality.

D. Squiggles can be relationship- or task-oriented depending upon the situation. Work hard, play hard is their mantra. Squiggles focus more on the creative aspects of work. Out of the box thinking, trying new things, and challenges energize them. Rigidity, detail work, dragging out implementation, and others telling them what to do or judging them drives them nuts. Squiggles can be confrontational, drop the ball on details, and jump from project to project without finishing the job.

3. Ask people in each corner to create a chart with two categories: one list with specific skills they bring to the team and another list for what they need from people with other styles.

4. Discuss how knowledge of each other's styles can enhance the team's work.

If you are thinking that each style should have their own team, think again. If each style were taken to the extreme, squares would carefully organize and implement what they have done for a thousand years with little innovation. Circles would be caring and fun but the quality of their work would be questionable. Triangles would have a high-quality research department and squiggles would have a super think tank but neither team would have much luck with relationships or implementation. It takes a balance of styles to create a team with exceptional ideas, good organization, and quality implementation without having people want to strangle each other.

What if your team doesn't have a good balance of styles? First of all, very few people see themselves as strictly one style or the other. Most people find two styles very comfortable and two styles less so. When a need arises, people are also generally capable of assuming traits that are not their primary style. For example, if Gail is a squiggle by nature but finds herself in a team where no one has circle qualities, she may have to play the role of peacemaker and guardian of relationships. This will take more energy from her, but maturity and experience allows people to flex and assume other styles when they need to. We gain energy when we are able to perform in our primary styles and we have to give more energy when assuming other styles, but either way we can make things work by being aware of what the situation calls for.

This simple way of thinking about human behavior is only helpful if people use it to analyze and improve relationships and productivity. It is not meant to put people into categories. Its power is learning how to capitalize on your own style and improve communication with people who have different ways of thinking and communicating.

Conclusion

What is important is seldom urgent and what is urgent is seldom important.

—Dwight D. Eisenhower

Careful attention to how you choose to spend team time can prevent rookie mistakes like these:

- Assuming that everyone agrees on the scope of the work and their responsibilities for it.
- Diving right into the work without agreeing on purposes, norms, and procedures for working together.
- Trying to do too much at one time.
- Talking issues to death when action is needed.
- Thinking that the work is more urgent and important than the relationships.
- Ignoring the need for ongoing and embedded professional development.

Masterful teaming requires a constantly changing and evolving set of complex skills. The big question we constantly heard was, "Who has time for building relationships and capacity with all of the other work being imposed from outside the team?" The truth is that no one has the time—people have to believe that building team skill is important enough to create the time to do it.

The essential elements of teaming must be firmly anchored in trust, competence, and reliability and must be kept in motion by consistent attention to norms and agreed-upon procedures. If there is respect and congruence between what people say and the way they act, you are on your way to maintaining a high performing team with all the satisfaction and sense of achievement that comes with it.

ASCD | arias™

ENCORE

ENCORE: TWO TOOLS FOR ANALYZING YOUR TEAM

 ## TIME-MANAGEMENT MATRIX

Steven Covey (1989) talks about a time-management matrix for selecting priorities when we feel we have too much to do. He says that our lives are full of time stressors that fall into one of four categories: urgent and important, not urgent but important, not important but urgent, and things that are unimportant and not urgent.

1. Urgent and important things have to be dealt with immediately because they are the daily crisis situations that keep popping up. For example, a crying student, discipline problems, team conflicts, or getting grades in on time are urgent and important issues. These are problems that must be dealt with immediately or they will cause more problems later. Urgent and important issues are the "putting out fires" part of education.

2. Not urgent but important tasks are things like exercising daily, establishing team norms and procedures, developing relationships, long-range planning, and professional development. No one gets excited about it if you put these things off because they do not feel urgent, but they are the ounce of prevention that keep emergency

situations to a minimum. Think of these things as taking away the matches from those who start so many fires. The ideas in this book are the not urgent but very important aspects of developing a great team. Ignore them and they will come back and set you on fire.

3. Things like sidebar talking, endless arguing over small points, confusion over who will do what, and FYI e-mails often appear urgent but do nothing to move your team forward in meeting important goals. These things eat up precious team time and don't ever pay off. Minimize them as much as possible.

4. Things that waste time like busy work, complaining, blaming, and gossip are neither urgent nor important and should be avoided. They clog up your team time with unproductive activity.

Make a list of 20 things your team spends most of its time doing. Where do these things fall in the matrix? How can you tighten up the way you use your team time?

SELF-ASSESSMENT: WHICH STAGE IS YOUR TEAM IN?

Here are some benchmarks for identifying where you are in the team development phases. This tool is adapted from Creating Effective Teams (Wheelan, 1999).

Stage 1

Can you state the purpose of this group as well as the routines and procedures?

Do people on the team know who you are and what you have to offer?

Do you feel like a valued member of the team with equal voice?

Are you clear on why you are a member and what part you will play in this group?

Do you have lots of unanswered questions about the "who, what, when, where, why, and hows"?

Do you feel that someone needs to tell the team what to do?

Stage 2

Is there confusion about goals, roles, timelines, and tasks?

Are there frequent disagreements within or outside of the meeting times?

Are people choosing sides or forming cliques?

Are some people just doing their own thing?

Are people jockeying for position of leader?

Stage 3

Are you clear on goals, roles, and timelines?

Is leadership shared among members?

Is there tolerance for differing opinions?

Is the team focused on the quality of their work and communication?

Do people trust each other?

Stage 4

Do members know and respect each other for what they know and the styles they bring to the team?

Are you proud of the quality of work your team produces?

Is there honest feedback and clear communication among team members?

Is the team analyzing their work and learning from their mistakes?

Is the team dedicated to helping each other learn and grow?

Are conflicts frequent but handled in respectful and helpful ways?

References

Blanchard, K. (2006, March). The critical role of teams. Retrieved from kenblanchard.com: www.kenblanchard.com/img/pub/pdf_critical_role_teams.pdf

Connors, R., & Smith, T. (2014). *The wisdom of Oz*. New York: Penguin Group.

Covey, S. (1989). *The seven habits of highly effective people*. New York: Simon & Schuster.

Gingrich, A. (2014, May 19). How to estimate time on any project (with the PERT formula). Retrieved from IDEASANDPIXELS: ideasandpixels.com

Larson, C., & LaFasto, F. (2001). *When teams work best: 6000 team members and leaders tell what it takes to succeed*. Thousand Oaks, CA: Sage.

Pink, D. (2009). *Drive: The surprising truth about what motivates us*. New York: Riverhead Books.

Sanderson, B. E. (2005). *Talk it out!* Larchmont, NY: Eye On Education.

Tuckman, B. (1965). Developmental sequence in small groups. *Psychological Bulletin 63*, 384-399.

Villa, R., & Thousand, J. (1995). *Creating an inclusive school*. Alexandria, VA: ASCD.

Wheelan, S. (1999). *Creating effective teams*. Thousand Oaks, CA: SAGE.

Related ASCD Resources: Teamwork

At the time of publication, the following ASCD resources were available (ASCD stock numbers appear in parentheses). For up-to-date information about ASCD resources, go to www.ascd.org.

Online Courses
Leading Professional Learning: Building Capacity Through Teacher Leaders (#PD13OC010M)

Print Products
Creating Dynamic Schools Through Mentoring, Coaching, and Collaboration by Judy F. Carr, Nancy Herman, and Douglas E. Harris (#103021)
Leading Effective Meetings, Teams, and Work Groups in Districts and Schools by Matthew Jennings (#107088)
Strengthening and Enriching Your Professional Learning Community: The Art of Learning Together by Geoffrey Caine and Renate N. Caine (#110085)

For more information: send e-mail to member@ascd.org; call 1-800-933-2723 or 703-578-9600, press 2; send a fax to 703-575-5400; or write to Information Services, ASCD, 1703 N. Beauregard St., Alexandria, VA 22311-1714 USA.

About the Authors

Marilyn Swartz has experience teaching at multiple grade levels in both special education and general education. She served as a curriculum director for many years and as a consultant for a Special Education Regional Resource Center (SERRC). She has provided professional learning opportunities for educators both nationally and internationally. Marilyn is involved in school improvement work with the Ohio State Support Team. In her current role as an educational consultant, she trains mentors for the entry year program for the Ohio State Department of Education, is an adjunct professor for Ashland University, and serves as a lead trainer for Searle Enterprises, Inc. She completed her doctoral studies in leadership and professional development and has a master's degree in curriculum and instruction. Areas of expertise include curriculum development, Marzano's research-based teaching and behavior strategies, response to intervention (RTI), intervention assistance teams (IAT), differentiation, co-teaching, and the development of integrated systems models.

Margaret Searle is the founder of Searle Enterprises, a consultant group working in the areas of collaboration, problem-solving, and innovative teaching techniques. She presents nationally and works with individual school districts to develop and implement continuous improvement plans. Margaret has been a teacher, Title I director, middle school principal, elementary principal, K–12 supervisor, and adjunct professor for Ashland University. She served as president of the Ohio Association of Elementary School Administrators and was an education advisor to President George H. W. Bush. Margaret is the author of the Ohio Department of Education's *Standards-Based Instruction for All Learners: A Treasure Chest for Principal-led Building Teams* (2004.) Her second book, *What To Do When You Don't Know What To Do: Building a Pyramid of Interventions* (2007), describes a step-by-step method for diagnosing causes of troublesome issues and provides guidelines for actively involving parents and students in problem-solving. Her third book, *Response to Intervention: What Every School Leader Needs To Know About RTI* (ASCD, 2010), and the companion DVD on secondary school RTI interventions are practical guides for teachers and administrators who want to build a culture of data-driven decision making supported by research-based interventions. Searle's most recent book, *Causes and Cures in the Classroom: Getting to the Root of Academic and Behavior Problems* (ASCD, 2013), reveals new neurological research about how underdeveloped executive function skills can cause poor behavior and achievement, and gives specific strategies for addressing these problems.